# ANIMAL LIFESTYLES

# Spinners & Weavers

### By Alison Ballance

## Table of Contents

Dominie Press, Inc.

# Introduction

Spinning is a way of joining **fibers** together to make them strong and useful. We get the fibers from plants, like cotton, and animals, like sheep. Weaving turns spun yarn into fabric. Most of our clothes are spun and woven by machines.

Animals also spin and weave. Some animals collect different types of materials, which they weave together. Insects and spiders use **silk**, which they make themselves. Different insects and spiders have different uses for silk. In this book, we will look at some of the animals who spin and weave.

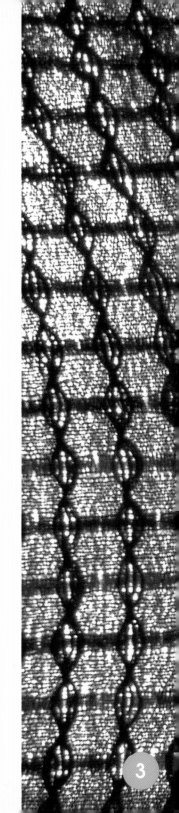

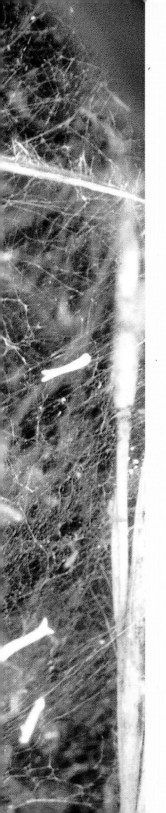

# Funnel Weaver Spiders

**Funnel** weaver spiders weave **dense** sheets of silk into a trap that they lay over the ground or over bushes. The spider hides in a small opening in the middle of the trap, waiting for insects to come by. When insects walk across the trap, the spider jumps out to catch them.

*Some funnel weaver spiders make traps that are three feet wide.*

# Orb Spiders

**Orb** spiders build flat webs shaped like a wheel. They hang their webs between branches. They eat insects that get caught in the sticky web.

*To make silk, spiders produce a liquid that gets hard in the air. Did you know that spider silk is the strongest kind of natural fiber?*

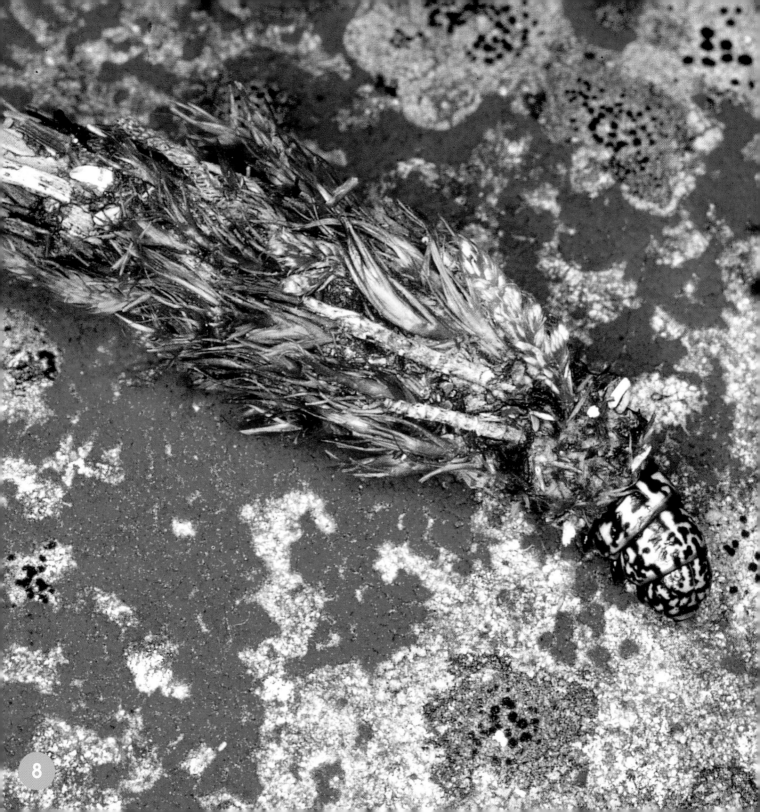

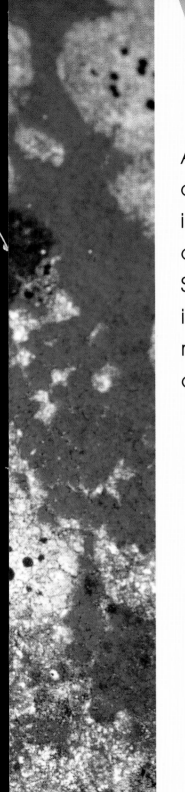

## Case Moths

A female case moth doesn't have wings and can't fly. She spins a silk case and lives inside it. Her head and front legs poke out of the case, and she can walk around. Sometimes she weaves pieces of leaves into the case as well. These leaves help the moth hide in trees. Predators think that the case is part of the tree.

The females of some case moths do not have legs, eyes, mouths, or **antennae**. They do not live for very long.

# Caterpillars

Caterpillars are the **larvae** of butterflies and moths. A caterpillar spins silk around itself to make a hard covering called a **cocoon**. The cocoon protects the caterpillar while it changes into an adult.

Inside the cocoon, the caterpillar grows wings and changes shape. After **emerging** from the cocoon, a butterfly has to wait a few hours for its wings to dry before it can start flying. Moths usually wait all day long for their wings to dry and harden, then they start to fly overnight.

A butterfly cocoon is called a *chrysalis*.

# Caddis Flies

Caddis flies are insects that live in water habitats. A caddis fly larva spins a case around itself using its own silk and small twigs and stones. The case helps protect the larva from predators.

Some types of caddis fly larvae spin a "fishing net" made of silk in order to catch small plants and animals for food.

*You can look for caddis fly larvae on the bottom of rocks in streams.*

# Weaver Ants

Weaver ants sew leaves together to make a safe place to hide. Worker ants hold the leaves together with their sharp jaws. Other ants hold onto ant larvae. The larvae produce silk thread. The ants move the larvae back and forth to make a thick silk **webbing** that **binds** the leaves tightly.

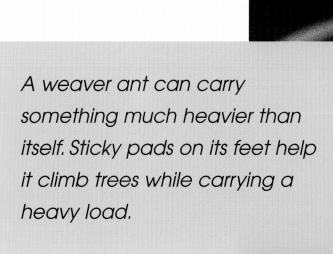

*A weaver ant can carry something much heavier than itself. Sticky pads on its feet help it climb trees while carrying a heavy load.*

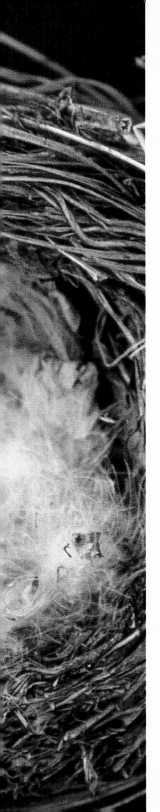

# Birds

Birds make nests out of all sorts of things. They use their bills to weave grasses, moss, and sticks together. Some hummingbirds even weave spider webs into their nests. They line the nest with soft things like feathers or wool.

*Birds like orioles and blackbirds use pieces of grass like thread, pushing one end into the nest and pulling it out in another place.*

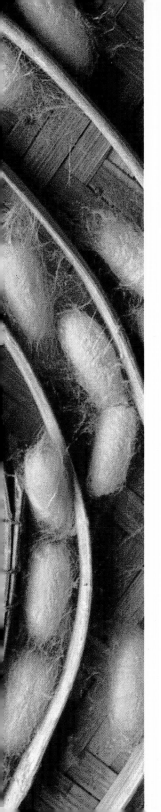

# Silkworms

The silk that people wear is a soft thread, but it is also very strong. This type of silk is produced by the larvae of the silkworm moth. The larva spins silk around itself to make a cocoon. The adult silkworm moths do not eat or drink anything. In their adult form, they live for just six days. The female can lay up to 300 eggs at a time.

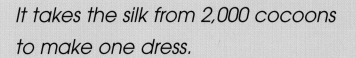

*It takes the silk from 2,000 cocoons to make one dress.*

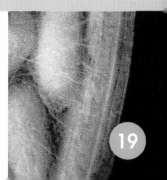

# Silkworm Farms

People have silkworm farms. They feed the silkworm larvae mulberry leaves. After the larva has spun its cocoon, the silk farmers collect the silk thread. One silkworm larva can spin a single thread of silk a mile long.

Today, silkworms **rely** totally on humans. They no longer live in the wild.

# Summary

Spiders and insects that make and weave silk have many uses for it. Spiders make houses and traps out of silk to catch their prey. Many insects make cocoons out of silk in order to change from larvae to adults. The cocoon protects them while they are changing.

Around 4,000 years ago, the Chinese discovered that silk was a good material for making clothes. They unwound the silk from the cocoons and wove the threads together to make silk cloth.

Today, people also use other materials for spinning and weaving. Sometimes we use different materials together to make clothes. Our clothes protect us from the weather.

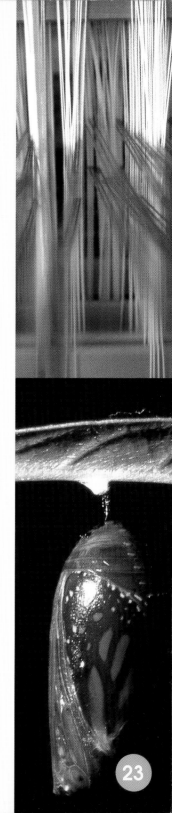

# Glossary

**antennae**   thin parts of an insect's head that help it to sense its surroundings

**bind**   to tie something together

**chrysalis**   a cocoon that butterfly caterpillars make

**cocoon**   a protective cover insects make around themselves

**dense**   thick

**emerging**   coming out of something

**fibers**   threads

**funnel**   a cone shape that has a large opening at one end and a small opening at the other

**larva**   the first stage of life in a moth, butterfly, or other insect (plural—larvae)

**orb**   a round shape

**rely**   to depend upon

**silk**   a fiber made by insects and spiders

**webbing**   strong material that is very tightly woven

# Index